WHAT AM I ?

The Story of an Abstract Painting

By Serena Bocchino

Revised Edition
Text and illustrations copyright © 2011 by Serena Bocchino.
All rights reserved. Published by *In His Perfect Time,* Basking Ridge NJ.

This is the first book of the Am I Collection Series.

ISBN: 978-0-9767674-3-5 (hardcover)
ISBN: 978-0-9838660-0-8 (softcover)
Ebook: 978-0-9767674-8-0 (digital eBook)
Library of Congress Control Number: 2011913046

Cover art: Landreach, 1993, oil and graphite on cotton canvas, private collection
Cover art available as a Limited Edition Print 2011
Available by the Am I Collection and Serena Bocchino

Graphic Design by Gayle Shimoun

For information regarding permissions or copies of this book, contact:

www.theAmICollection.com
www.serenabocchino.com

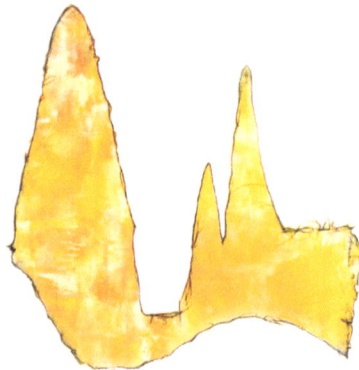

Special thanks to my dearest Stephen, Ezra and Rachel Keough, for their support and inspiration.

Thank you to designer/artist, Gayle Shimoun for her creativity and fantastic
design sensibility. Her friendship and understanding has been invaluable to this project.

Additional thanks to Elena Bocchino, Jill Kastner and Jill Stein for their encouragement.

Printed in the United States of America

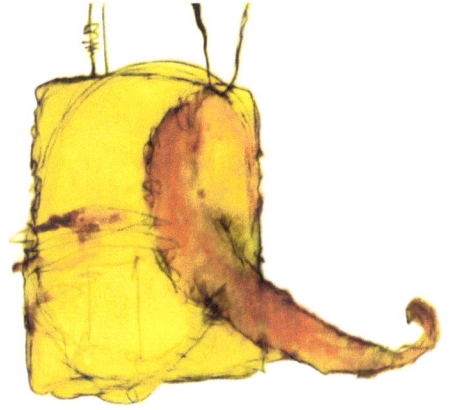

For Stephen, Ezra and Rachel

The space was empty.

1

So Yellow came.

2

Yellow filled the space.

Yellow wanted company,

4

so he invited Structure.

Structure did not want to miss a thing,

so he made Windows to see out of.

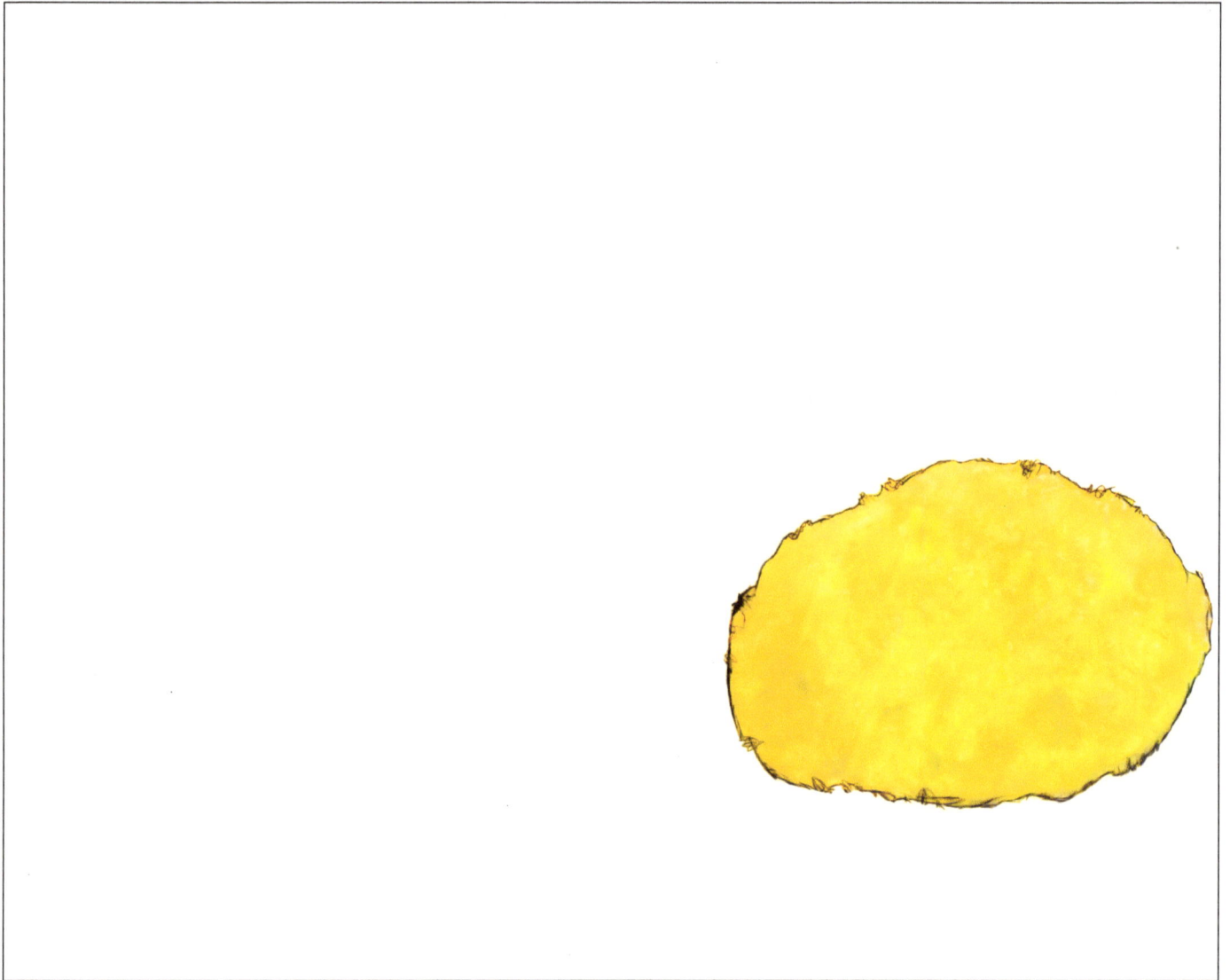

Structure wanted to have a neighbor,

8

so he asked Shape to join him.

Shape said, "yes"

and decided she would be a Pond.

Structure became very happy

and it showed.

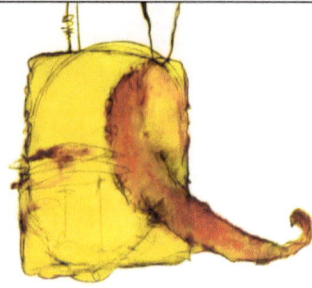

Sun and Moon were invited too

14

and hung around with Structure and Pond.

15

Sun and Moon reached down to Structure

16

and they held his hand.

Wind came...

18

and added pink to the sky.

19

Suddenly... Wind blew parts of yellow to white

and the sky was now... yellow, white and pink.

And Pond

became blue.

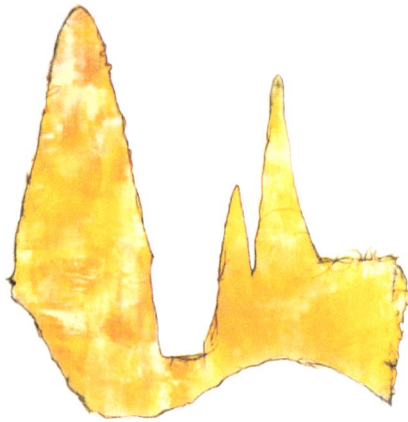

Mountains were watching from a distance
and wanted to play.

So Structure invited them.

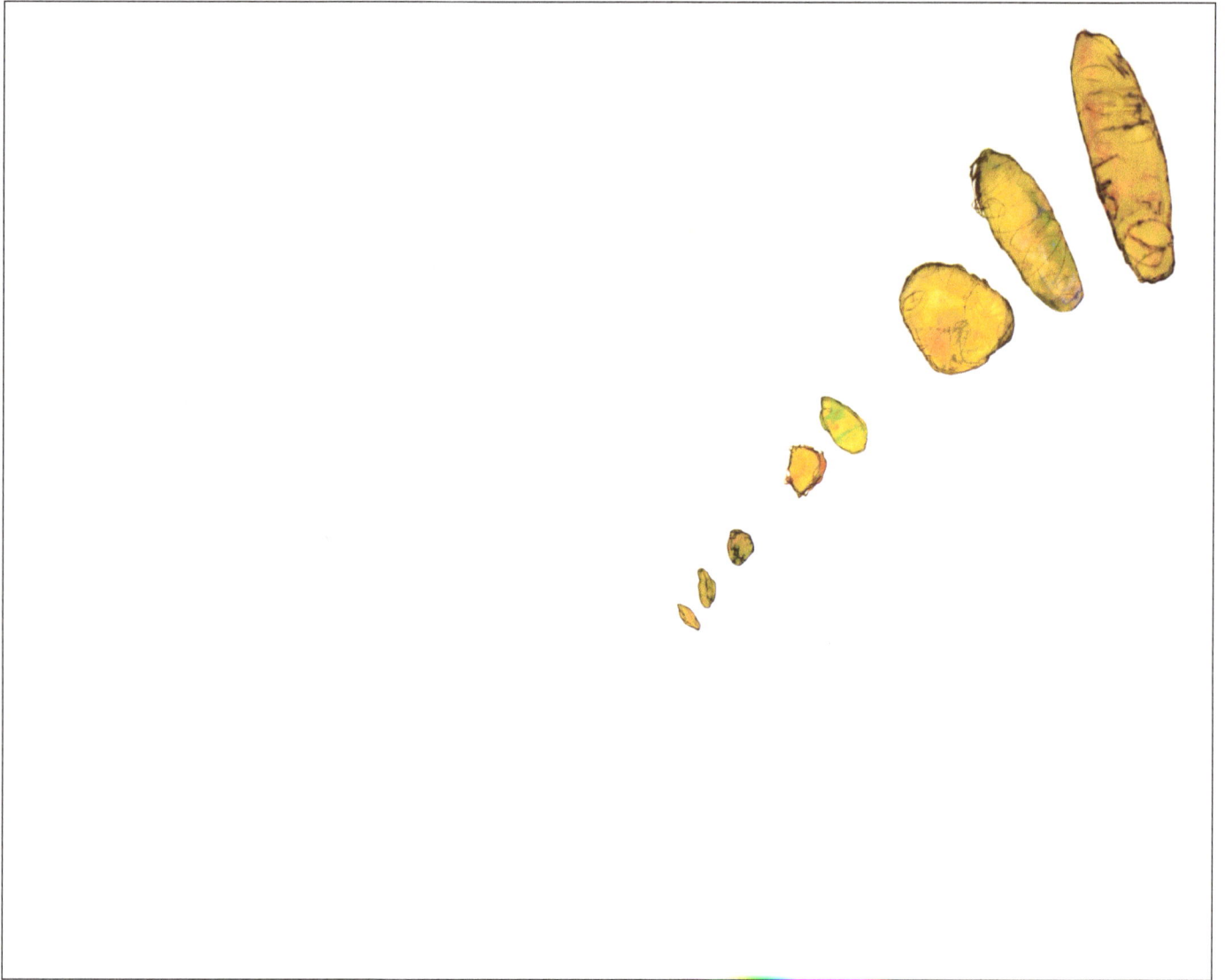

The Circles followed

26

and joined in the fun.

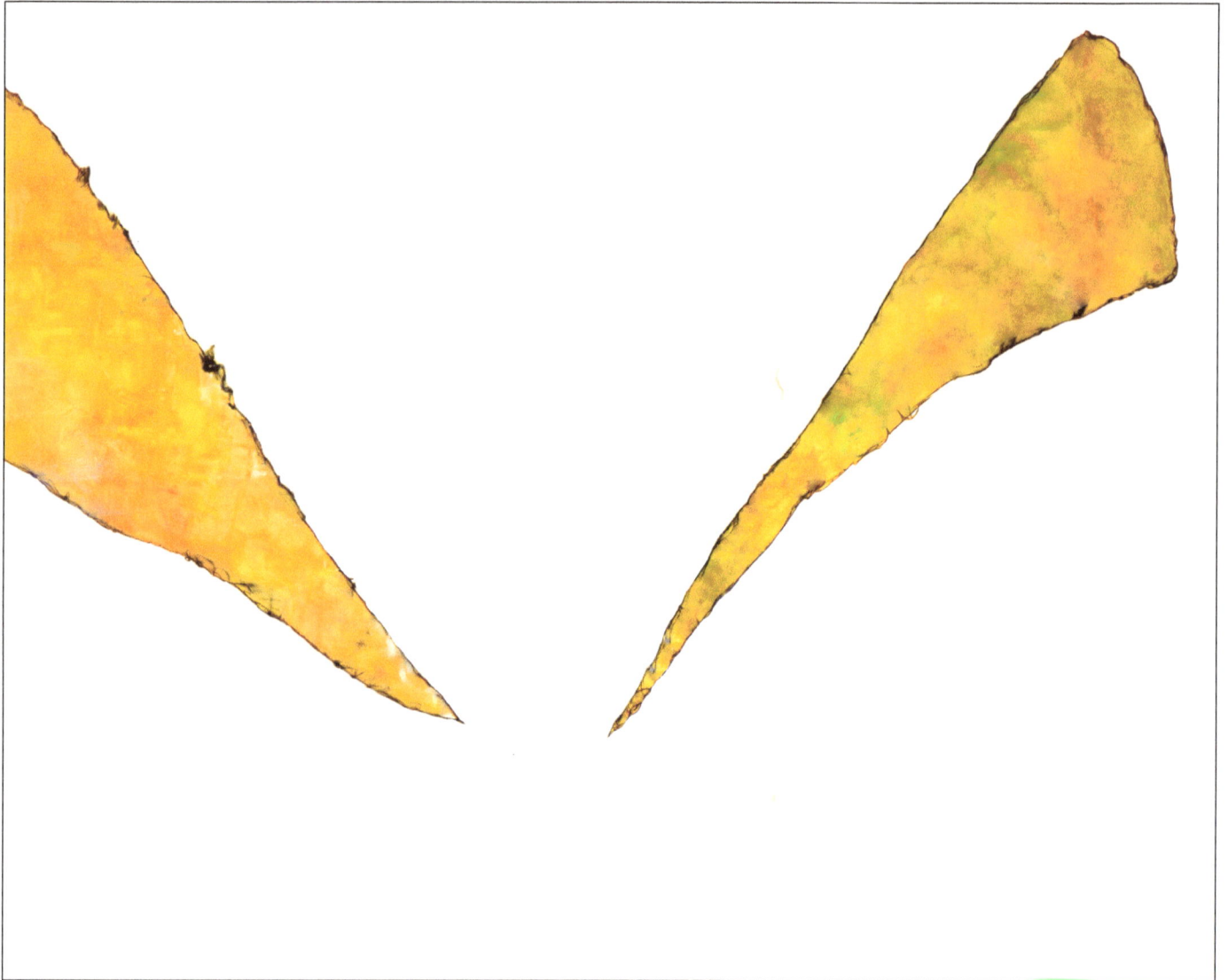

Structure was so happy to be with his friends

that he reached out wide and hugged them all.

Art from the Heart

Fun Art Projects For You to Make
All you will need are crayons, colored pencils, or markers.
Choose paper and use the ideas listed below.

One Line
For this project, remember:
Red's complementary color is Green
Blue's complementary color is Orange
Yellow's complementary color is Purple

Using one crayon or colored pencil, color the whole surface of the page evenly. Then, make a drawing using a single line using the complementary color. Do not lift your hand off of the page while drawing the picture. Even when you draw objects that may be in separate areas, continue your line to connect them making sure your hand does not come off the page. This is called a "continuous line drawing".

Two Lines at One Time
Begin to draw with both hands from the top to the bottom of the page. Try to continue to draw at the same time with both hands. Next, try coloring in your drawing with both hands. You may want to experiment by turning your page upside down to color in areas. Relax and enjoy the process!

Five Lines with a Friend
Draw 5 random lines in pencil. Have a friend use a colored pencil, crayon or marker to connect the lines to create a picture. Fill in the areas made by the lines using colors and shapes to complete the composition.

One Line and Seven Shapes
Draw 7 shapes on the page. The shapes may be different or the same. Color in the shapes. Using one line, connect the shapes. As you pass through each shape, create a small drawing within the shape, then continue on to the next shape. When you are finished, you will have 7 drawings inside of one big drawing!

Lines, Color and Pattern
For this project use colored pencils and remember:
Primary Colors: Red, Blue and Yellow
Secondary Colors: Green, Orange, Purple

Create a line drawing with a black pencil. Fill in half the shapes in your drawing with primary colors of red, blue and yellow. Fill in the other half of the shapes using secondary colors. In three of the shapes, use your black pencil to create patterns such as dots, stripes, stars, or squares. Now look how "full" your drawing is with lines, colors and patterns!

Congratulations, you are now a promising young artist!

Serena Bocchino is an artist who visually interprets many different subjects ranging from music to nature to the urban environment. These rhythmic and energectic paintings are an investigation of abstraction and color.

Ms. Bocchino has a Masters Degree from New York University. She has earned awards from many art institutions for her work including New York City's Artists Space, PS1 Contemporary Art Center and the Museum of Modern Art. The New Jersey State Council on the Arts has awarded her fellowships in both painting and drawing. Her work is included in prestigious international private, public and corporate collections.

This is Ms. Bocchino's first book in a series about abstract art for children of all ages.

To see additional artwork by the author please visit www.serenabocchino.com.